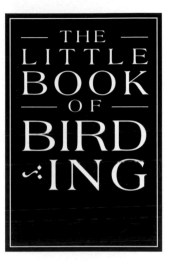

THE LITTLE BOOK OF BIRD ~ING

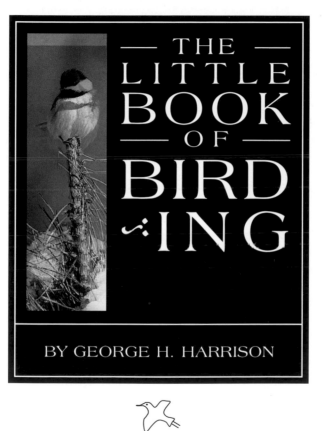

THE LITTLE BOOK OF BIRDING

BY GEORGE H. HARRISON

Fitzhenry & Whiteside
Markham, Ontario

© 1998 George H. Harrison

Licensed to Fitzhenry & Whiteside Limited for exclusive sale in Canada by arrangement with Willow Creek Press.

Fitzhenry & Whiteside, 195 Allstate Parkway • Markham, ON L3R 4T8

Published in the U.S.A. by WILLOW CREEK PRESS
P.O. Box 147 • Minocqua, Wisconsin 54548

The Little Book of Birding was conceived, edited and designed by Willow Creek Press.

Design: Heather M. McElwain

All photographs by the author except: Maslowski Photo: pages 10, 11, 19, 22, 24, 27, 45, 56, 57, 60, 62, 73, 83, 88, 89, 98, 99, and 105; Duane Manthei, pages 48 and 112; Kit Harrison: page 68; Hal Harrison, page 69.

Canadian Cataloging-in-Publication Data

Harrison, George H.
   The little book of birding

   Canadian ed.
   ISBN 1-55041-376-7

   1. Bird watching. 2. Birds -- Identification I. Title.
   QL676H38 1998   598'.07'234   C98-1930653-4

Printed in Canada

This book is dedicated to those whose lives
have been enriched by the sights and sounds of wild birds . . .

ARE YOU A BIRDER?

If you love to awaken on a spring morning to the dawn chorus of robins, you're a birder.

If you are warmed by the bright *wit-cheer, wit-cheer, birdie, birdie, birdie* of a cardinal on a dull winter day, you're a birder.

If you admire the energy of a tiny chickadee cracking sunflower seeds, you're a birder.

If you get a kick out of the hoot of a great horned owl at midnight, you're a birder.

If you smile at a male house wren nearly falling off his perch as he bubbles with song, you're a birder.

If you marvel at the orange in a Baltimore oriole, the red in a scarlet tanager, the yellow in an American goldfinch and the blue in an indigo bunting, you're a birder . . . and then *The Little Book of Birding* is for you.

— George H. Harrison

CONTENTS

THE
BIRDS

Birds . . . they are with us from dawn til dusk,
from the red-winged blackbird's sunrise *con-gor-ree* . . .
to the screech owl's *whinny* under a full moon.

Birds fascinate us,
whether they be everyday birds with ordinary feathers . . .

. . . or once-in-a-lifetime birds
with quite extraordinary feathers.

They entertain us,
whether they are winsome . . .

. . . or homely, young or old,
they are all on stage in nature's grand theater.

We marvel at their grace and elegance . . .
their flight.

We are struck by their majestic power and cunning . . .
and their exquisite jeweled beauty.

They captivate us when they are coy and shy . . .
they intrigue us when they are brash and bold.

They grant us the pleasure
of observing them in their familiar haunts . . .

. . . and the thrill of spying them
in the secrecy of their wild domain.

We are awed by their adaptability
in an ever-changing world,
and their perseverance in the renewal of life
year after year.

We are touched by their parental dedication . . .
their nurturing of the next generation.

We rejoice when we see the young of the year,
new life to reassure the continuation of the species.

At home,
we feel an intimacy with our garden companions,
as we view the world of nature through a window.

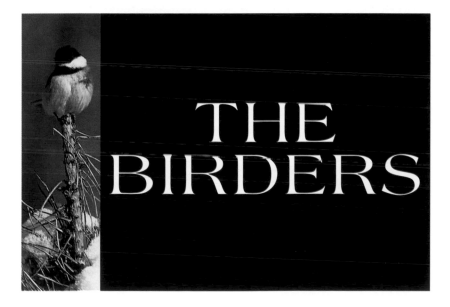

THE
BIRDERS

We birders are a gregarious lot,
often flocking to our favorite places
to watch and be watched.

Yet we often seek solitude,
quiet moments when we can reflect on life
and our place in the great scheme of things.

Like the birds,
we are usually
well equipped
with the latest and
most efficient gear
hanging from our necks.

We band them, study them,
and gather scientific information about them . . .

. . . while wondering who is studying whom.

Fledglings in a wide world of wonder.
To begin birding at an early age
assures a passion for birds for a lifetime.

Some of us are as vain about our bird watching . . .

. . . as some birds seemingly are about themselves.

Sometimes birds and birders
get confused about one another . . .
Which one are you?

GREAT HORNED OWL

We love watching birds,
not just for a day, but for a lifetime.
Never boring, never tiring,
our quests are eternal.

We are always sharing and caring.
Whether in a city park, a wilderness camp site,
or a backyard, birds come first.

Birders migrate too . . .
at times we travel far and wide
in search of new entries to our life lists.

Birding to the ends of the earth is exciting,
but deep down,
we know there's no birding place like home.

No winter is too cold,
no summer too hot,
no spring too wet,
no autumn too dry . . . for birding.

Birders stand out in a crowd . . .
our uniforms so varied, yet so distinct.

GREAT BLUE HERON

Birding is a sport
that combines the best aspects of hunting and fishing.

BIRDS THROUGH THE SEASONS

Birds carry us through the seasons,
bringing us joy in the depths of our winter doldrums . . .

. . . and the promise of new life and revival in spring.

We offer them gifts to fit the season . . .

. . . to lure them into our lives.

In early spring,
we anticipate the arrival of birds from the South . . .
an act of faith.

Yet our faith is often rewarded . . . as new life debuts.

Legions of birds return from afar,
destined to reproduce their kind . . .
in the high rises we provide,
and in the duplexes they improvise.

We reward the migrants with sweet offerings,
in return for their song and dance.

We welcome one and all . . .
each color, species, gender, shape and size.

Well, almost all . . .

We design our yards and gardens
with the birds in mind . . .
food, water and cover.

Birdhouses for cavity nesters . . .
trees and shrubs for others.
If we build and plant them, the birds will move in.

NORTH SHORE OZAUKEE

DUCKS UNLIMITED

Some birds can't read . . .
others aren't particular.

We dare not judge the perfect clutch of eggs
by the housekeeper that laid them.

Kids will be kids,
no matter to which family they belong.

But sooner or later, every kid must try its wings . . .

FLEDGLING AMERICAN ROBIN

. . . and take that first flight into the scary world beyond.

INDIGO BUNTING / NORTHERN CARDINAL (LEFT); AMERICAN GOLDFINCHES (RIGHT)

We offer bird baths to lure them from cover,
for close-up viewing while they drink and bathe.

Splash. Splash. It's a bash.

Clean feathers, clean feathers, and off they dash.

We mourn the losses —
so many don't make it . . .
with windows to hit, hawks to escape, storms to dodge,
starvation to avoid, and sickness to ward off.

Autumn brings renewed excitement —
migration begins for some . . .
food storage for others.

Soon the migration is in high gear . . .
with birds of all sizes, shapes and colors
heading to warmer climes.

We wonder at their remarkable journeys . . .
tiny hummingbirds cross the Gulf of Mexico . . .
snow geese to the tundra . . .
arctic terns traverse the poles . . .
albatross sail the endless seas.

In winter, birds gather on feeding grounds,
ranging from vast wetlands, to huge rain forests,
to modest backyard feeders.

Survival often depends on finding food
early each morning to sustain the body
through another bitter cold day . . . and night.

Feathers are fluffed to retain body heat . . .
the heat produced from body fat.

Open water in the frozen North is a luxury
that can pay dividends in the form of rare visitors.
The cold declares its own dividends
when wandering travelers visit backyards in search of food.

So, we're birders.
Off the top of your head,
do you know of a more fascinating pursuit?